JONES VERY

JONES VERY

Michael D. Snediker

ORNITHOPTER PRESS   CHEVY CHASE

First Edition

Published by Ornithopter Press
www.ornithopterpress.com

ISBN 978-1-942723-17-2

Library of Congress Control Number: 2024934971

Cover image:
The Blast (Portrait of N), 2018
acrylic and ink on canvas
© Henry Chapman
courtesy of the artist

Design by Mark Harris

for KBH

CONTENTS

Walk, with personality.

—Lloyd Price

⁂

To date there is no inventory,
only the dream, though I remember them.
I remember the rocks.

—Roni Horn

JONES VERY

I.

INSTAR

I bure thy Grace upon my bak.

—Sir David Lyndsay

CAMPO APERTO

If the geranium girds again. The ewe in its urn, the farewell fibbing in its head. Far cries from a self, the diligence of what doesn't absorb evolving. Perfoliate numquid sown in the gladdened. In swaddle rangling a well-placed smudge on the filament. The nova moth welling, the distaff this. The two of us taking turns in the scene's scant metabolism. In the allergy & how the parchment shook, irrationale cutting in. The ravine catastrophe misunderstood as a comedizing mist. Neither action nor speculation but a middle eye raged just then in sedge. Off went its wig with the feelings of a bird. Either this or he flinched aloud, the powder of making himself perceptible. Now comes the explanation. Where does the music come from. Should you like to go elsewhere. The light in the cord. What I meant was stars. Headlong this morning in question, our last seventh sphere as love to the mossy pot. In the wall, where it was hidden. Hither hinder sunder when I was a child of pale green sky. Come wrung from it a crown of tamarisk. The sibyl's village lost to eventide each time. Lesser bee-lines of spirit movement, shipwreck learning to be still. A shadow quarrel freezing over the field. Were we solid when you came to the sea. At least an orison. It blew right through me, the morning sings, its fossil beauty. The thunder in the ark straying hollow beside a leaf. I copied his little cave of anger. What have I to do with wishful emergency. Say again about detachment, the jasper light in my eyes. The Swedenborg of morning fretted away.

COR CAROLI

When I was lifted into the radium.

A fringe plume inlaid with
conversational stammer. Fished skittish

from
the petal-cloth, a crease
in debt.

Rosewood & the idea of a movable jaw in cuticle silver.

Ego stopgap as an impasse

salvaged from clouding & conducted as a quiz through the hearsay

of our formerly
transponding selves.

—

How I courted that tenderfoot in
bursts of mishap, sulked

teeming into the floor or
paddled out to moot point—

bashful & spent-ebb
as another
me.

—

Wherever we perseveratingly went the magpies
of magnalia yondered.

Our resin apostle's unheard
of blindness

wearing out
this coat, carrying

these arms.

The reprieve from inwardness wasn't as
expected, feigning

as we did
not to be involved
any longer.

—

Stunt monochromes of wind &
a cold boomerang of change,

a rook
in the cuddy.

Hesitantly the future
returns as temperament quailed
in distant entropy.

Negligent miracle, in this capacity
I was fogging over.

Squalled in the shell with
you awaft.

—

Stabat rubric.

This gumming of anecdote
pries our abandonment lesson

from the tines.

To sing him the weight
of a drone swath inkspot

off in aperture, in
exchange for steadier
piers.

Before the line
becomes a space in madder.

—

Vandal whetstone come-on cruising
an ode in the new

barn.

Wakening a weakness for rough pigment.

Whatever the story belonging somewhere else, a newly scouring
travail in the wool of inquiline.

—

I saw as the skull whose cradling couldn't anything anymore,

than this erratum of arrows.

A fontanelle at any rate

where the deer
nearly spired.

—

An oblique place be-
mazed in waves, a pulpit afloat
in the impasto moat.

Was it Tacita Dean or Saint Jerome
who sealed our ships against

the desk dark scarab of law,

optical bareback briefly fed
on pulse sparring with
what was left of

the arabesque.

—

The outer seagull's ever
fainter geotaxis.

—

A bagatelle a bagatelle a face
like the agate
morn.

A felted face-like quibble.

—

Having drunk each noon his utmost
vegetable health.

How we justified his cliffside masque

catching in
the tunnel rust.

—

So we creep again
through the dove-

house, again
this house-

broke shrine of trance in tender.

Stretching the glove to bury the phoenix
figment on swallows hinge.

What was concord to the warm
sutra of will, this intimate

vagrant anyway gathered at the tasseled edge.

THE FUTURE OF FRIENDSHIP

A young man weddyd to the kyng lost his ring
climbing from the Scantic river,

borrowing names from

maps of fountain later scribbled
from his Amsterdam
of bed.

—

They found the hole
in the ice through

which the martyr spoke.

What they predict in
its mouth &

see there

waging bottomless
scorch lark
fiction.

The moon's expiring
paragraph pulling our ankles
down

to the sea in self
defense.

All those meditative stinkbugs elegized
in windowsill pollen as we
burn away.

What language wasn't snow
angel structure cozened
from the drift.

—

Duraflame. Cheerio.

What Ray Johnson kept there
left in Locust Valley.

The minor materials of his celery heart doubling
over the boulevard & down,
the flash

of flesh redistributing as rain as
the thickness of his film diminished.

Worsting the ego's
extra vowel.

Tucked in like manner into the nervous,
the prism's hunger
strike.

—

& the bird's choral talking cure take care take
care trenched in the vein,
where an

I collapses as
diagrammed through

a veil.

—

This is a description of shivering my body asleep in the catalog.

& this is a transferential undertow snagging both sides of the batten.

Deep in the dappled, a glaze misalignment harboring some shared
idea of breath.

—

Undertow of several
wet-eared minds

lest its substrate figure resurface
in pinchbeck.

Having lost thread-
bare to it alone.

—

An uncreated shine & the secrets of
a river stuffed & strewn, to this

end with
this illegitimate siphon,

its
reckless plainsong spills,
spilling in,
into

some zodiac of
unpreparable place.

Kimono of sun &
an exoskeleton of qualm as he
leans in.

The nautilus of his groin
roped in the Shaker chair.

& now his massive animacy,

from the ring to the wax without
leaving the ring.

A sharpie & 7 across
his chest.

Where your cool hand had been.

TWO KINDS OF CARE

When we'd seen as through his face the last of the scavenge. Harpsichord algae repeating wood for tree in the sodden. Where someone's rough-spun might a little bit wash off. & practice bees overheard in the spangling. An heirloom feeling or algal equivalent. Asemic organs for kicking around the gloam, taken to swim then tiptoed through an obscure courage sap. Travertine, the quick fugue gesture of his luminary legs a shoulder shoaling beneath the cylinder of his shadowed rib. An animal, in short, in the nimbus of composition's absconding swarm. The honeymoon knocked all over with riddle garnet amiss in lattice. Residuum of lions adream in crib lily pulver. Victor Hugo is said to have carved the furniture through the mask with his teeth. There will be no more eclogues today. Listless seaweed errorist & pillow diary. Here's an unsolicited collage of skyward panic, a low room of anemones. Whose compartmentalizing weasel mouth sometimes puts forth a sward. Of disputed buffoonish brightness, who wheezes binnacle & frequents listening thicket. Wax foot coverslip courtship hatch in a swell. A milder liveliness mulling where the abridgement glitched. Going bingo in the park, a sheet of pearl at a level line, a bed of grief sunk into itself like Flemish star oil. Gladiolus, the trapp rock over there. Who could sleep with all that chrysalis. Should it chase me flat against the star-eyed wall. Its maker met in a godlet cage, the sepia boy abyss. My own.

HOVERING TENDENCY

This time really tell them I go for it.

I can't. Go on.
Like this.

Into the damask,

btwn buttonholes of
bellwether health & the feedbag
of its cautionary tale.

To the hills & all.

For the shield of
his last good wing cupped shimmying
to the barrow.

Ruck maker held
dotingly to the air's surprise.

—

How sicklyk our lyfe.

—

The mater hapnit thus so ragged & rent.
Dungeon here, dungeons there.

The morning after my departure, the day after
my death, I wept like a child grown
busy with absence.

Determined to embrace it,
I did embrace it.

& just as we understood
each other, as it
floored me.

I made my mind
up like a bed.

—

Hedged in the wistful parafoil of his smile.

My next heart whistling a broken window

following the echo
to its cell.

Where I was guarded, I insisted, the cherub conundrum
for which my spider solitude
rejoiced, the web

it fed on.

—

I wrapped my head in cloth despite the drum of heat.

Tinder polypore. Hoof conk. False tinder
polypore, the bugbear of his arms
about my neck.

Shrunk from dishevel
& in this way

learning wisteria & six-wing clamber.

Two bodies placed
beside the one
dissolved.

—

Neptune & nacre.

Cohibiting sediment of an askebathe.

I was the jailer holding sky.

An acrobat's refusal safely attributed
to birds blue beads
fastened to

the forehead of
our hounds escaping through
an opal plaque.

—

Six groats & a pennyloaf fed to a cave
& there we stayed, capsized in
clay. A flimsy curtain

btwn us &
the bardo basin.

If Neptune, paid
in samovars at the door.

—

A song for the quarry, a soft
shoe prayer.

In the twig work dream he cuts my throat.

A silkworm doubt eased under violets &
blue gauze tremor in
grotto snow.

Circle iris & blue

as Agassiz once admitted in a grove.

—

Wavering in the matterhorn how

I tried to tell
an atom from a heart from far

enough away.

Should you sift from
the strum an eddying gloss of
offshore light.

Our poor paraverse, they will say.
Coarsening the coal.

What remains of kerbstone bezel
deepest kept, the locket's

clippity-clop.

II.

EMERSION

You should have seen the fields go—Gay little
entomology! Swift little Ornithology! Dancer, & floor, &
cadence quite gathered away, & I, a phantom, to you
a phantom, rehearse the story!

—Emily Dickinson

WHIG FEELINGS

Pathos dew & not there.
Acorn & a plot of moss.

Oh when will night crystallize in you again.

Also is an acquaintance in the red array
of accident that was the work. An artificial heart.
An artificial sea shall make

ascesis of you
yet.

Snow across a barn or beauty from a dust.

I sleep now in the bushes, the bureau
angels burgling. A polite
bed of

mint rose rises in the boat without
beholding.

Cloud milk pulls.

My brain for another neck &
tromp as writ. For when

affection clogs, clinging timidly to avalanche.
This exercise of isolated comets.

An anodyne for moth.

Forgive me the arrogance,

he told me.

Permit me to accord with your abler machinery.

I was disappointed & celestial as
sleet while you went away.

My awkward life. It ascends,
bride of the precipice, the stars bedecked.
She came halfway home.

THE NEAR CONTINUUM

Of mercury glass
attachment & spiral buckthorn.

Low lying displacement of
pines by stars of

foster myrtle a few miles off.

Carrying camphor far as its steadying
slant allows.

Night-blooming declines of kind
& votary the very

notion now a catafalque
covered over.

Perched in
the formula's bryony cope, its neglected
rime.

Fernfelt.

A colony hand being guided through lakes of
wind lifting gently as on
a soft shield.

—

If buckthorn pines
for place as sleepers in a field.

Briar marvel harbor

& sleep's fickle pattern dissolved in
shuddering white.

—

Filigree
centurion.

Cardinal catkin gold.

—

What arrests colonizing gentleness isn't
the petrified medium
in

its orrery sky.

—

Somewhere btwn swans
divining themselves when we

come around
alone &

rescued from the blinking.

What pearl in this pest of brain
would dream such
green

twig formalism
more than
once,

such terse spells of bridge
behavior.

CONCORD & MERRIMACK

Interview is acres.

A clouding adverb in the furlong
of our sameness & the trial
enough.

Pollen eleison, a bank done
in by pencil

to acknowledge mesh.

—

Continually putting off
becoming leaves me bare & charred.

Hand-me-down, like
a night releasing its tetanus
of oracle.

I want a clover & have just clover to offer.

You called me wayward, reaching
that conclusion,

picking
up these stems.

—

My Sitwell birch pronounced as cannon
& deathless as Emerson's "squirrel."

Five eggs on the sill & little wells dug but never filled
appease the retiring bell's pink errancies.

The psaltery stain.

—

& trees of vapor filling to the brim. The vertical
fugue by inundating degrees.

Heady with delinquency I crossed
lilac to ward off wax
doll scholars,

a summer dog noting down the sky
with tongs—

a watchcase, a fortune-teller.

The celibacy
of scry.

—

A bureaucratic child carefully
redacts his
fort.

Half-mast chrysoprase,
tallies of gaslight—

& everything within sight within reason hastening away.

—

Clothe me with goliath
in the estuarial fade.

To say the emblem, a lower elm circumference
in milk-palm prose. Whittled
from slumgum

cumber to
a key.

—

An onyx finger in a museum of salt takes fire.

& the fires, elf of rapture,
begin again on a flocked shelf.

Underlight, those Roman dog habits least
preserved in endocarp or
graver quill.

Requited, scratched in passing.

A watery
stone as viewed from
the rafters.

PILGRIM OF ELATION

Moon gate, master of nets.

A prow of grace in the sheep's baffle.

Some remove
from the trellis it happens, she says,

a cyclone fermenting
unremarked.

—

The scarecrows lean & loaf.

Bribing
the witch elm.

Polyphony dogwoods awaiting
evidence of absence
at bay.

—

The beekeeper spanning his softness when

the pilgrims return with their pensive enameled hands.

—

The change came about this way:

a depleted tutelary
lozenged in concentration.

Content in
the decorative sense.

—

Somewhere in the overlay skulk
six pheasant mysteries

startled blue in
the sumach.

Darting just so, palette
& gangplank
pounced

in the weld.

—

But I knew, I thought, I stray.

—

All the squandered estrangements
more or less restored.

Larceny of angled
garden evenings in loops of bale.

My mob grown
smaller & his

words gone hazarding.

A loose botany in the weed sleeve of
description.

TRUMPET FLOWER FEELING

A wishbone squint-hole's oxidizing hum. Twilight haggling on the wing, in the friezy hills. A sorcery hover in shingle histories of hoax sulfur. Concussions of sun leave us loose paraffin, an old straw disobedience wooed in tremolo. The itch of us before sinking back stretched thin. We were strongly built, but this. Each arpeggio tare, faint efforts at rearrangement. Wash cloths buried in the wall & thunder borrowed from the rift. A violet truce btwn kingdoms resurfacing as the machine we sorest needed. Btwn your inclining rind & my wan declensions. World enough for a cross of crevice things, entering the cloakroom through a lotus of unruffling thought. Blanket gesture, bulb mystery—braced against the law of turning eaves into ornament. For braving tar paintings from the nineties. Their haggard fine print of impinging aftercast. Lingering there in the alley ardor. Our shadow box of friable treasure orphaned in the whiplash. What wants. Just calm enough to press the eye into remission, or light. Love a duck resuming lettuce duty as though recovered from the first trilling hint of alarm.

IT IS GROWING DAMP

& I must outrun the nuns. Somnambulist with
a mouthful of pinkish scrid: I should never
have returned to

this world.

I say there are images thrown off
the bodies of
objects.

The pellicle swan brushing the pupils gently,
a dark air hit hard in the sternum keel.

Atoms atone the spot was there & the bright dots

were there all along.

—

Plotinus says nature roughs out living
bodies but it is the pendulum
that goes

missing, the cyclamen of its
tongue.

& alone it was the sculptor alone chosen by lot,
a sphinx wandering far from her hive.

Nobody yet believes save the calico fern.
My saints, I could have begged them to

stay becoming air.

—

We look alive in azalea
swale & numb to the etiquette
of admonition.

& so the dream of a vast intimacy

begins
to vanish,
taken into the wane.

Hoping a little drift, horizon in hand.
Together on high gray rock.

Come back, pirate, I can't.

—

The cowardice of strangers on a little fence,

dividing their devotions
accordingly adorned.

We hemmed the crash. Sent
it across its ravenous
fraud forgiving
fond

with octagons of triage from
the sugar in our marrow fist.

STREGA NONA

Go in old thorn. Apple to salt
& spikenard.

A last-minute accident in the mill of attention

from
boy to hollow boy.

Fig in mordant, nymphs in
amethyst crying out at our expense.

The aura btwn them a little addled.

For days now thimbling on pyramids dredged in shadow
lavender.

Quickening, the glacier
moon over which winged things wandered fog
in rutilated fog.

While others grew from the feathers shed
in moss pond meadow ponder.

But only the smoke
survives, amber
thatch in Benjamin water.

I live there in the factory of a feather
wristed voice.

In a vision of peacocks waking to alchemical rain.

Forgive this charlatan his green glass grain for eyes, leaving
their paste on everything we claimed
to see.

The chaudron chatter in the leaves, sailors
in slow motion straining from all
that open.

A serpent girt with his watery heart
& wax conscience,
bath-robed or

pressed into turpentine.

I wasn't always meanwhile made of wood.

I stole down like snow in
common water.

The error now is all
I own but

how the creasing
floods away,
the blue

crow bar of
our mouths.

OPENING HAND

When the compass calyx when.

An echo returning
to itself becomes a twine of song.

Having scrounged against this thing before, whether or
not being haunted by grace feels
like grace.

The body's uncoil as an inscription of stammered air.

If I could feel as I see
this sepal effort.

When one wears a cobalt performance
henley as one does,
trying

near midnight to make one's
way down a winding
path.

Down which years
before some old halcyon cracks

a bicycle into oblivion.

Sepal imprint.

How we were undone
from the branches, having crashed
or grown together.

A cherry tree, an elk-
like elm bending its antlered
head to a stream

in Attica.

A basswood or linden sprung
from the hollow of
its mother

like a screwball misgiving transformed
over time into wiles of aware.

How they cowered in this fashion
over someone crouched
below.

A child or forest when it finds
itself adjacent to an oblivion,

like battered starlight or
Chappaquiddick.

When sound at it most urgent gives
way, the breath knocking back.

You went searching for a dancer & found
a dimming. Absently spiraling,
you rehearse yourself,

like the door in a chime.

MINOR POETS OF THE CAROLINE PERIOD

Weather man rubicon. Disturbance pageant. Our impression of his benimbled noise. Who sobs in numbers. Dabbling incognito fountaineer. Apostrophe ruins & our sooty throat. The prank in its veins. This winter something of its yew-&-roses charm. It left me flagged in lichen, howling like the lighthouse in a mowing field. Some crazy altar brood-spot, that kind of dazzlement. I didn't want to pitch my pain is hymn meter swindling. Prop bouquet, survival headlamp. Softer flux, I wasn't used to feeding my relation to object relations. Here comes the train. Or balanced on the balls of our foreshortened feet. No art more gossamer than this. My rogue slowness furlough, where blew a wilder time. The spandrels down, & filling the nerves. If they would only stay. & stop these postcards from the clingstone prairie maze. My perplex circle of wet. Dull to temper advice. Once learning to write through thaw. Arguing overcast the long way to Westerly. An arm of sable plums clean off the map. Somewhere sails, an underlying quadrant. My best friend riff. If in mulch revel, how she heckles the exode by its chafe of umstroke. Groomed for the mock moon's plot, a prayer wheel in ragweed. These shambling hands. Thus spun the hiccup computations. Some other point until the earthquake slips. Into view, into the learning curve. Its meteor kiss.

GLEN COVE

Apotropaic hydrangea
slingshot or
Orphic

drive-in of lessening
presentiment.

The shadow of
which whatever
it is

seeps like blue-flag in a bog.

Knitted into quorum,
a humoring fuss
in

the kiln of grain.

—

Moving away
moving
away.

—

An idle thread &
no word yet

from the blear
temple presto of all the old

unfoundlings, their stark veriment

pooling
past my tent.

—

If we did this, subsiding.

If it went no further than
the agitation, the
poem

having taken
the place
of something else.

—

The pearl in the ear of the sailor in the port.

Disappointment on a post-romantic cake.

—

& then you bring me the first
frail surface, a wholly imagined libido
to return to the ballyhoo.

Repeat after me.

Your repeating interest.

—

Sweet-talks in half time shot over the prow.
Niccolite a vein in slate.

Pink is
cobalt bloom
scarce spinel transfixing his

bevel face.

—

His sorry voltage,
a blossom in lapis perigraph

pored over on the commuter train.

A bull-eyed shelter busying
itself with charade departures written
smooth

then rough. Some uncouth
swain of concern beside itself

on the lookout for
fidget weather
looking
in.

—

Watering the reliquary
ice-tooth to its very canvas.

Some Arnold or Ava
filling the tourniquets with
saxifrage.

—

A map of soap, his singlet
delicately put.

Ditto
the Brontë

faun its cinema of
blush.

My small umbilicus,
its sieve shorthand in the sapphire
patch, his

hazel in a bare place.

—

Bark jewelry,
lintel clarigold.

An engine deep in the woods of
Emerson spooks my narrow inner

shoulder like a throat
to trillium vigil in
the round.

Having pieced together our
competing ransoms
as we could.

More sphere than hoped,
dispersed in halo
ebb.

& emanating in good time
from the barely.

III.

REM IN RE

But when the angels saw me they fled, & said to one another,
'What portent is this? How did this bird of night get here?'
And I actually felt myself changed from being a man,
although I was not changed.

—Emanuel Swedenborg

REM IN RE

Goad credo whether quaver or
my larynx season of wilt.

Our cleverness hard & unkind sinks
into the parable, he says.

Disposed, supposedly (he continues),
a continuous body sent on
its way.

An artery arrayed
in edgrow.

—

Shaken twice self-
hooded, so
soon

the jewel's small
awe discarded in the good bye tide,

our little dinghy thrown
voice-like under
the bay.

—

Lemon
series. Dim-spent
dispatch

shoremen
crimped to the merry ship.

We were frontiered & afraid nonetheless,

having so long
delayed.

—

Mr. Cocking did not fall out of the wicker but
with the machine, the hole in the middle

had it not
collapsed his
parachute of cloud.

At length a theory a tarn of
plunder stirring devotional crosshatch.

A jam in the wicker
trussed oblong.

Confinity, the balloon exhausting itself.

Our neighbor with his arm in the valve.

—

Preamble the place

where time was rope or
feeling mizzened with yesterday's

intimated rain.

How the slurry vertex
hardened nobody nightly.

Bulwark a gaunt sanity in
chrysanthemum the
instrument

tripping downward,
pooling—

a self
grown round.

—

His studded Byzantine
scrivening

the grime, sliding into each other.

An architrave we,
devoured twice.

—

This is what we did
for celadon, this, the rumor

of my favorite mother on
the subway story

dissolving as
we speak—

an amorous detour sent further astream.

More sculptural.
More hole.

A pretext for one last meeting
indefinitely frilled along.

—

It's hard living down the tempers without
a grammar's loose diplomacy
of sleep.

I was so inside the other sentence
once emerged from
the girding of

the breaking
up machine & miles of string.

One day to clarify
my body's axis improvised within
a pulp.

—

Elaborately.

Rotting where we crept
back to the gouache.

—

Go ask her.

The victim detail, a seahorse keepsake
sown with burrs in the wrong
manner.

Dreg song on the outside

of its own
hasty body on the outs as
we all

preferred.

—

Sooner run from the bargain we think to ourselves.

Alloyed whereabouts unknown &
pedant jetty jawing,

unknowing its range.

Templo-turrified in bloodhound chalk.

—

A brisk formalism eats the lakes
out of iris. A bit dark.

A little blue-scribbled battle with the conduit.

The trouble wasn't
loneliness alone,
my secret emergency

mode enough walked back
from the begging
day.

—

Three red stars fossilize in
the schoolyard a rhododendron

insomnia tinting the sweet
of pursuit.

We have no brick nor garnish daddy—

how we
address each other in
the liquefying room of the snow-
globe's gathering
fret.

If timber's easy kernel.

The huntsman vexed was also
stone defensively spoiling
the root-meat.

—

I shall cede, I cede.

A plague in the pippins.
Some scalding bristle from the trough

of a late morning
tub.

—

& the marrying whip-quote

teased from
your water-hedge,

a school of realism descending
one last time—*koi*
koi

& anniversary flint for smoothing over
the deluge or whatever this mirror
warning answering

in fluke echo
was.

—

Selling the cypress
& privately, the flabbergast.

—

The absorption I'd always
wanted. Sparingly.

The coping of his noddled head.

Trample lunge
chant & forge owl cabbage

where the door

keeps ajar, tussie
mussie cosmos staring
the easel back.

—

How the phantom
limb gets put

to use.

—

A spasm of fraying purpose
in the winter midst,

where the swimmer in love swims
under, removed from

the pain
scale for good
behavior.

—

Afloat in permission, silver mar
of sleep in its chain,

a suspension of
salts bored through cork.

—

Aisles of bronze in a wooden cloud & then

a settlement

of goldenrod spread far across these hills

turns gray.

Pestle thistle, a bruise in ormolu to soften lacquer.

Shell lac still the split-light twig.

—

He seemed to be describing
the very underpass.

Our clinkered bird's
inharmonium.

The dockyard's roving prayer &
knotted as a sailor's
child.

—

The yarrow & tansy of it all.

Longer lawed the leaves
of azure meander

reciting burgundy
burgundy maroon.

To the miniature herd
astonishment pulled furrowing
from the well.

You are nobody's
Nero now.

—

Should the last pressingness approach
with its autocrine of downcast
questions. Isinglass,

ego in escrow—where
my dune
hollowed friend
roughly

speaking countersigned—just think on the lull. Pocketed, the four of them.
Terribly, I loved them all.

IV.

& Scene

For shape is a trace of the shapeless; this
then generates shape, not the other way around;
& it generates shape when matter approaches.

—Plotinus

INTERFERENCE FRINGE

Our ceramic boy still
pansies in the little dell.

Everything in allium my twilight sallow seldom.

Having eased from
the grid another fable of

he'd been the girl
all along.

—

We were nine & counting the syon
cope of his mind's eye, something
left for the expedition
& beside.

I'm trying, the cosmos says.

Just shy of an endurance
installation

pouring the warble in both
directions—whale moat mostly
combed from

the gild mud up.

Singeing the edge cone
obtrusions of

a bearded
iris.

This iris newly heavy in its cup.

—

The swain in pain sways mainly in the rain.

If it fused, if it stayed
his purple
wings. Shaking

the so-called swerve music
he swallows wildly
like a key.

—

Regular in the Jamesian sense, the scenic

route unkenneled right up
to perfectly parallel

faces of a spar, a dowel
of prase

in the lungs's thunder-
coil green.

—

These properties of bodies once
so gingerly beneath the waves.

Something flowing at
the point & something going
slack.

Consider a flywheel slowing down.

A delph ensign. These too are types
of privacy. Interiors of heat

lightning.

A family of twinning quartz
weathering out the schist.

The ambush of our mostly granular
being adrift in perfect
happiness kissed
through

the mirror hours.

Alexander in his A sutured
btwn phosphorus & sterling
periwinkle

in a cylindrical box.

—

I'm trying to tell you about a falsifying
satisfaction, the disquiet
omitted.

The child's rejection of quaternary membrane.
The fifth a child of porphyry rage & sponge.

Other cases I have lost lost to private record
& scant, a brooding homeopath
cut clean clear.

Aconite & last resort for
a waitsong pock
mercurially passed away

as the oarsman from his oar.
I was its wilderness, his middle term.

Analogy was
the intimacy, his way

of holding in
the haze.

ANOTHER GNOMIC DEPARTURE

Numbering the sparks. Oculist offense of snow-light bragged in the yellowish sand. Here a hylodes, a reddening of scrub. Staghorn still aglow in the prime of its charge. For whom I wear this indigo of restless. My emerald dynamo of error. On the derelict quay where we vitrified. A cabal in charcoal overcome with garret ivy, burin in hand. As if by telescope. The varnished dark returned to its spirit lamp. In silk the clotted sky of his festooning brain. An angle of coppers rounded off & a prince in disguise. Restacking the pears, what he heard in the air. Pornography of sunsets btwn the erasure of allegory & an umbel of birds. Still lives of foxed books. Is it fun. Is it easy now that you know how. Were we enclosed in a hex, the same brocade of pause in gemini. Montjoy narrows & totem smoke. A mirror resembling rain, a splintering surf made do with shanty armor floating away. Away in ailment. A receding intimist outlining this change. The tendencies of a canal. How you keened to return to the Necker cube, sea-worthy in six places. Where we plundered the star-chamber. Wedge beetle planting cinders in our yard six inches long, should you perhaps become again our guest. Arbor labor laid aside. Turning on castors, confused for stellæ. The canto of your thumbscrew meddle. Ten candles lit where there were two. & her preference for the house aflame. To whom ribband hark in passing. Hurly-burly on the deck. I was fished from the Acheron, having tried to make a hole in space. I'd lived in stencil. On a syllable. My tender supernal city plunged in a tub. Tugged verbatim into the orpiment. The use of hard relief; the mechanism that held us up.

NOT FROM NON-BEINGS

If it were reasonable
& the lengths I went to

pacify far past
their bachelor's dune or
sanctum foam–

alveolus by the Faustus sea flowering
a specimen of disagreement, the more piercing
geometries long buried in

the studio.
A fading shed.

A George Brent festival recovered little
George from the loam.

Wobbling in
his upper third, a vicarage
in the vicar.

Corolla of arrows
giving our orbit the taste of
a man-shaped bruise.

When you become a verse, on the ground.
Armscye, formerly a man on foot.

Now bulb now. Making for
nervousness,

the seawall sweetness left

behind a flowing
cry far from

the sawmill. An enclosure of meaning
ruminating our stippled face.

Any nowhere at all.

We found him in the crook
of a crab-apple. I looked around to see if he
had gone & this is what
I saw.

Nailed to the door. The rattling of
a brook. & this is as far

as we ever got.

There is an easy light now in your head,
a mirror we'd never seen before.

Lobster buoys hung to dry in a blaze
of agaric. Albedo up to your very shoulder,
the dodo silhouette of its favored claw.

How far from Needham, her banner
seamed to the mast.

The cadence of intervals having hatched
another visionary hunger.

Crystalline as backwood
madrigal,

a fine sieve
no-

show withstanding scrutiny

& lightning
rods for all that affective
noise.

GRASPED AS FOLLOWS

Withstanding rust in celadon (blue-green spiral in the slope).
Withstanding sentiment (hinterland honeycomb
flagging).

My style of combustion is

perfunctory decline (penciled lightly in).
A lowing shallow value in the chromatic sense.

—

As the blueprint quickens, as we summon
surface tint alphabets
of larva drying in a rare cold.

—

Fawn-down radicals at the least
touch run together, held to
the glare.

Lycoperdon radiatum in thriving ruin,
a meditation on

the flock of a breeze-
way wall.

I felt so copious, more or less
scattered on
the interior as discerned

by a roving

mushroom light.

Enough.

To fill a chariot
twice—

—

I was forced (retreating, to reach)
land. Land hyphenate, this

was not the case.

Pontormo séance pergola under which the poor
man's manna soaked for days stirred each night
a petrichor of vex,

regrouped for
dear life behind the charter
oak.

—

One step removed from carpenter consciousness
the given vortex drops. A point without length

approximating an object, restless from the story &
its storying world.

If we did so, those Quintilian days,
a triangle nearing
spring.

—

The comforts of spoiled substance

culled from berm scrap braided together.
& a photograph's colluding heed for the curve.

Remit to sky what
the ghosts had set aside without
the wall, a wall-

flower's promontory
silt.

—

An anonymous calculus underwrites the throng at
long last uncertainly afloat, eked by the neck.

A faucet for the hermit & velvet for
the hermit's
goat.

Scuttling in the on
& off & my better half hawked

for all this blanketing
blankness,

the dizziness of living so aloof in
an ornament's gash of corrupting gold.

FIRST HAND EXPERIENCE

Coward fairy where
goes the goose-
written,

moons of pressure basting
themselves in.

I am a sky striation, now a Stingel
foil mumbling brakes into
the notch.

—

Anticlockwise,
a stubbled understudy
attrition.

Smuggling into the gulf
archive sketches of the next
world's sassafras.

Thatch derelictions
of a rowing pine.

Suppose somewhere November

houses & forests getting in
the way, almost in tune with
the oil.

The falters of which one is apprised
months after infidel & hoarse alone.

—

Syntax mercury dowry mine.

An unfamiliar sheepishness
cauls the dawn. & all

the loosely episodic
inroars: rose
mortise, bricolage.

Sobbing dew &
friction runing my relinquish

all
the way home,

comet neon down
the fledge-
path.

—

So we were being
borne in mind.

Seven trials conducted
the results of which left us shaken. I am
shaken now stranded

in the Jupiter wrack
of a plumb line's plush.

We become the tarot for better

visualizing the trouble fast
approaching.

Having taken that liberty,
our black hole euphemism.

—

A phantom rawness where
I was envelops the coast like a crying fit.

Child hush rock arms. I would gladly
lay it down, winnowed
into the welling

where the fears let in &
the gale veer
keep,

which kept recording
what it was.

INDUCED NEUTRAL

Retiring, I shall not follow him
to the winter schoolyard nor

the lakes where the pistol missed a second time.

Shrub casualty.

I shall not follow rills being
newfangled & largely here.

—

To be worked on, he took

his shirt off & I did the same, the materialism
of which felt like nothing at all.

A coarse gingham where the gravel
had been.

—

Another word

for babble, a peal of praise
from the ash pot was also coupling
alchemically

speaking,

a muffled tone chucked
from the coreopsis.

We looked it into the world.
Leaked into it.

Peaked in.

—

A catapult's minimum
condition, a deserter's self-devouring
edge.

The work of sharpening
emptiness with a jeweler's vast.

Our puppet-loving
mischief,
avid & deciduous

in the candle lapse.
A silk spy

spotted in
tallied lavender
time.

—

I will condole, I said, in
some measure.

& immediately the head
bends,

a cardboard tambourine
in the armistice of an underestimated
hand.

—

Was there just this one courage,
its conspiring huddle.

—

A man shall not be a pond.

Covered in snow,
wending his wean.

Someday I shall be so
grateful an object & inconspicuous
as

the raven surviving
its collation.

A bezoar of dignity, something like
intaglio entrusted to
then

brushed away,

the chestnut mutations
storing up.

—

See how the glove of a cloister border
wheels my merlin chair across
the library over

this harsh
of invented lawn.

Did we want a gentle or a careful god.

His gruff interest
distended, faint
fretwork

for refunding the husband.
Should one come to pass.

—

The people he will know, the illegible

motto round the lip of his dusk
in the hull.

—

Hazy receding inkstand &
strange: I walk in the garden, I think
on the paint,

the whirr you become, precisely that consistency.

WAKE IN ANAGRAM

What is held over time learns a softer form.

The loosestrife & its pagoda of bells.

I might lose myself therein.

Paper (under the paper floor).

It shall not be a law.

How long will we be buoyed in encaustic.

Clerestory harbinger, its mulberry verb.

Appearing as through a needle end.

This time was different as later it would be put.

This history of the diagonal.

Where its terrible stasis slogan began.

The voice's hard pine coaming coax.

Music box tendon on zenith drone.

Some queerer shine.

People die a little to break up their style.

Let a man eddy thus.

Decorative realism, the veto meaning of.

Finial, half-forgotten.

Tulip parabola & his beloved spiral.

How we found them turning in his grave.

Defray a dumbshow for unpromising sea.

The hem of anchor & potter's wheel in pamphlet.

Despondency scattered in the crowd, lifting along.

The cygnet of my dreams grown old.

The bull-calf of its heart.

It wanders the milk promontory bit sideways like an herb.

The octavo of intervening years in its tail.

Something like a tail, swung side to side.

Vigorously practicing on other objects.

What objects in what are not quite our hands become.

Acclimating to the dolphinarium, the moonstone parlor.

Red-lit dolmen omen domine done over.

Model families btwn the third & fourth escarpment.

Still feeding the typewriter organza.

A chicken wire glitter.

Eyelets in anchorite carrying dust in rivulet.

& mustard for the cornered fox.

Cuneiform a frog in clay where the sick were tended.

FOR EXAMPLE THE DOVE

My melting cap afish my arms
were raised &

there you are again

re-unioned on the bier,
the burning pier running fast as we can.

My stalemate of remorse as
scowered from a frieze. In a swamp
having cried

kitty-kitty long enough.
Swamp garden
swamp,

where we found the gypsum thief
pinioned to our sickroom
of belated floor.

In the dub glow smear of motionless angels thus &
thus unfolding like a fan's rosette.

—

Cappadine,

what the rabbit
thinks & what the fat.

Draw a church of geese
feeling with a char pendulum

laminated for
support.

—

Owhither well &
ozone music.

Unlike the cockle the nettle
opens. It swells by
degrees.

The flag in the maze.
The maze of our crest,

five shy trinkets in a row. Fragonard
& brain stone pink petrified
the sun each

day described as
milling over our heads.

—

A coffin at perfect
peace, they said,
a science but

not a science in low meadow laid.

The carapax of certain
crabs answering the net.

—

Its almost
familiar inflex.

The spirit too
disbelieving in
its stall.

When they use the term force
the ache of things
outside

themselves tries to steep away.

—

The morning in question. I woke full of ice.

There were ways, his sweat
dream curling
on the cricket ladder.

A nursery distress pledging a torch
mistaken for a cloud no
bigger

than a hand.

Uneasy in my aster
litany as though one could surmise
much less

assent to harpers in the spar,
a hearsay elation's incunabula.

—

A boast of bandaged animals drops from the graph

reenacting the source
of our leaning in the doorway pose
like electrons just now

emerging from
a storm.

The amount of light it travels &
what it contained of
the diaries

of wild Alexander.

Prying (trying to
pry) his life

apart from
the apparatus.

—

Herkimer howleglass
& whom, our

library of under
water oaths
choked
up.

Once
there was a weed
that mimicked brink wasp betony but

never again
half lifted

curfew singing
here is archery but

soft.

NOTES

I do not believe school is from schola viz. σχολή, but the Teuton word meaning
assemblage, collection, as shoal, a school of whales
shell (in a school of form).

—Gerard Manley Hopkins

"CAMPO APERTO"

"Campo Aperto," the open field. Adapted from Willi Apel's *The Notation of
Polyphonic Music 900-1600*. "Neumes are called cheironomic (staffless, in
campo aperto) if their writing gives no clear indication of pitch; otherwise
they are called diastematic or heighted."

"THE FUTURE OF FRIENDSHIP"

"From the ring to the wax without / leaving the ring," attributed to Augustine,
cited by Duns Scotus, *Concerning Human Knowledge*.

"TWO KINDS OF CARE"

"Victor Hugo is said to have carved the furniture... with his teeth," adapted
from Ned Rorem's *Paris Diary* (Autumn 1956).

"HOVERING TENDENCY"

"How sicklyk our lyfe," adapted from John Bellenden's translation of Boyce's
Historiæ Scotorum (1527).

"The mater hapnit thus," adapted from Sir David Lyndsay's *The Dreme* (1528).

"Dungeon here, dungeons there," adapted from Silvio Pellico's prison memoirs
(1868).

"CONCORD & MERRIMACK"

"& deathless as Emerson's 'squirrel,'" adapted from an 1882 letter by Emily
Dickinson to Elizabeth Holland.

"PILGRIM OF ELATION"

"Darting just so," adapted from an 1870 letter by Emily Dickinson to Louise &
Frances Norcross.

"IT IS GROWING DAMP"

"Plotinus says nature roughs out living / bodies," adapted from Henri Bergson's
The World of Dreams (1958).

"MINOR POETS OF THE CAROLINE PERIOD"

The poem's title is borrowed from a volume of the same name, edited by
George Saintsbury (1921).

"Yew-and- / roses charm," borrowed from one of Saintsbury's footnotes to the
poetry of Henry King (1592-1669).

"GLEN COVE"

"Written / smooth // then rough," adapted from John Crowe Ransom's
account of Milton's *Lycidas*.

"REM IN RE"

"Our cleverness hard & unkind," adapted from Charlie Chaplin's "The
Dictator."

"Mr Cocking did not fall," &c., indebted to William Upcott's *Scrapbook of*

Early Aeronautica (1783).

"Hard living down the tempers," adapted from Gertrude Stein's *The Making of Americans.*

"Lawed the leaves / of... meander," adapted from the journal of Henry David Thoreau (Oct. 15, 1851).

"Templo-turrified," from Joan Evans's *Time and Chance: The Story of Arthur Evans and His Forebears* (1943).

"INTERFERENCE FRINGE"

"Something flowing at / the point," adapted from P.W. Bridgman's *The Nature of Thermodynamics* (1941).

"ANOTHER GNOMIC DEPARTURE"

"Bragged in the yellowish sand," adapted from the journal of Henry David Thoreau (October 2, 1858).

"Clotted sky of his... brain," adapted from Diogenes Laertius's understanding of sperm as a "clot of brain containing hot vapor within it" (Michel Foucault, *The Use of Pleasure*).

"Is it fun. Is it easy now...," adapted from a 1944 letter from Fairfield Porter to his son:

> Darling Laurence:
>
> Mother said you can really swim now. I am very proud of you.
> I couldn't swim until I was nine so you see how early you learned.
> Is it fun? Is it easy now that you know how?
>
> With love from your Father

"The mechanism that held us up," adapted from Aby Warburg's "The Theatrical Costumes for the Intermedi of 1589" (1895).

"GRASPED AS FOLLOWS"

"A point without length / approximating an object," adapted from C.S. Peirce.

"INDUCED NEUTRAL"

"Covered in snow," adapted from Walter Benjamin's "On Some Motifs in Baudelaire."

"A man shall not be a pond," adapted from the journal of Ralph Waldo Emerson (1845).

"The whirr you become," adapted from Stepháne Mallarmé's "Little Ditty," trans. E.H. & A.M. Blackmore.

"WAKE IN ANAGRAM"

"The loosestrife & its pagoda of bells," adapted from the journal of Ralph Waldo Emerson (1842).

"Paper (under the paper floor)," adapted from the journal of Ralph Waldo Emerson (1842).

"People die a little to break up their style," adapted from the journal of Ralph Waldo Emerson (1842).

"FOR EXAMPLE THE DOVE"

"Howleglass," the hero of German folk tales, for instance, "How Howleglass was kidnapped while he was asleep in a bee house; how the robbers left him, and he became a gentleman's servant," or "How Howleglass broke the chapel steps of the holy monks going to sing matins, and what ensued" (*The German Novelists: Tales*, ed. Thomas Roscoe, 1826).

ACKNOWLEDGMENTS

I'm indebted to Yaddo, where this book began, and whose holding environment is gift beyond measure. My thanks to the following magazines and sites where versions of these poems first appeared: *Action Spectacle, Black Sun Lit, Blazing Stadium, House Mountain Review, Interim,* and *Prelude.*

And all vast gratefulness to Lynn Callahan, Elaina Richardson, and Christy Williams; and to Branka Ársic, Dara Barrois/Dixon, Henry Chapman, Lucy Corin, Colin Dayan, Marianne Ehrlich, Jared Daniel Fagen, Molissa Fenley, Ethan Fortuna, Elizabeth Freeman, Latria Graham, Kelan Nee, Bevin O'Connor, Brittany Perham, Katie Peterson, Peter Richards, Leslie Roberts, Eleni Sikelianios, Courtney Stephens, Cole Swensen, Daniel Tiffany, Roberto Tejada, Karen Weiser, Mathew Weitman, Hiroki Yoshikuni. And to my family, especially Quinn, Knight, and Austin. And to Louise Glück, whose early, generous guidance has made the rest conceivable.

Last but not least, to Mark Harris, for responding to these pages, and for giving them a home. And to Kevin Holden, for whom they were written, and who makes so many things besides more beautifully possible.

ABOUT THE AUTHOR

Michael D. Snediker is the author of *The New York Editions* (Fordham University Press, winner of the Poets Out Loud prize) and *The Apartment of Tragic Appliances* (punctum books, Lambda finalist for Best Gay Poetry), as well as *Contingent Figure: Chronic Pain & Queer Embodiment* (University of Minnesota Press) and *Queer Optimism: Lyric Personhood & Other Felicitous Persuasions* (University of Minnesota Press). He is the fortunate recipient of multiple residencies at Yaddo, and is presently Professor of American Literature & Poetics at the University of Houston.

www.ingramcontent.com/pod-product-compliance
Lightning Source LLC
Chambersburg PA
CBHW022157080426
42734CB00006B/477